S0-AAD-670

Smotherly Love

I Know Where Your Buttons Are and I'm Not Afraid to Push Them

Debi Stack

Published by
Thomas Nelson™
Since 1798
www.thomasnelson.com

SMOTHERLY LOVE: I Know Where Your Buttons Are and I'm Not Afraid to Push Them

Published in Nashville, Tennessee by Thomas Nelson, Inc.

Thomas Nelson, Inc. titles may be purchased in bulk for educational, business, fundraising, or sales promotional use. For information, please email SpecialMarkets@ThomasNelson.com.

Published in association with Janet Kobobel Grant, Books & Such Literary Agency, 52 Mission Circle, Suite 122, PMB 170, Santa Rosa, CA 95409-5370.

Some names in this book have been changed to protect the privacy of the individuals involved.

Library of Congress Cataloging-in-Publication Data

Stack, Debi.
Smotherly love : I know where your buttons are and I'm not afraid to push them / Debi Stack.
p. cm.
ISBN 10: 0-8499-0198-7
ISBN 13: 978-0-8499-0198-0
1. Motherhood—Religious aspects—Christianity. I. Title.
BV4529.18.S73 2006
248.8'431—dc22 2006037675

Printed in the United States of America
07 08 09 10 11 QW 9 8 7 6 5 4 3 2 1

To my mother, Beth Lawson:

a pianist, a poet, the world's best cookie baker—
and a woman who still gets the giggles in church.

Contents

Acknowledgments

Thanks to Beth Lawson, my mother. You fueled my wordsmithing from childhood with books, library trips, and magazine subscriptions. You paid for speech therapy when I was in grade school so I could speak with confidence, a car in high school so I could stay late for journalism, and my first typewriter in college so I could write everything from term papers to poetry. You've always been there so I could do this. You are awesome.

Thanks to Elizabeth, my daughter. You blow me away with your eloquence and editorial insight. Your writing in this book is fantastic and funny. I can hardly wait for your bylines to surpass mine. You are exceptional.

Thanks to Neal, my husband. Your love language of service—from shipping books to assisting at my speaking gigs to refilling my printer with ink cartridges—is a constant encouragement to me. You are extraordinary.

Thanks to Andrew, my son. Your amazing artwork and hilarious sense of humor give me endless joy. You deserve a T-shirt that says, "The farce is strong in this one." You are inimitable. (Go look it up.)

Thanks and thanks again to my book club, lunch bunch, and other supportive friends. You are priceless. (Though I wanted to mention you each by name, my editor said there were too many to include here. She also nixed my listing of all the books I read during the writing of *Smotherly Love*, the music I listened to, the meals I ate, etc. Check out the unabridged acknowledgments at www.debistack.com. Another reason to go online: stuff for daughters on how to deal with their picky, clueless, stubborn, bossy, and dramatic moms.)

Thanks to the steadfast pray-ers around the world who lifted me up and carried me through. You are blessed.

Thanks to the mothers and daughters who related their stories of smotherly love to me. Sharing your voices with women and girls around the world is bringing laughter to us all. You are delightful.

Introduction

Join the Party!

No one can push your buttons quite like your mother can.
After all, she's the one who installed them.

—Anonymous

Welcome to the world of mother-daughter drama. As every girl knows, conflict between mothers and daughters is as old as dirt and almost as fun.

So if you tell me that you and your mother (or your daughter) never butted heads, locked horns, or argued, I will be forced to accuse you of being in denial.

"But, Debi," you may say, "I'm not in denial."

"Yes, you are."

"No, I'm not."

"Yes, you are."

"No . . . I'm not!"

"Yes, you are. And apparently you also have an anger problem."

"NO, I DON'T!"

"Oh, that sooo proves it."

We've all had conversations like this with our mothers or daughters. Back and forth we go, debating until our blood boils. The topic may be curfews, hemlines, or something of true life-or-death importance like the merits of a three-quart saucepan.

Why do we do this? Psychologists may postulate about power struggles, but coffee-cup wisdom says it all comes down to love. It's simple. It's complex. It's emotional. It's a choice. It's gone. It never really left.

Smotherly Love is all of that. It's the poignant mingling of pride and loss in a mom's heart every time her baby girl reaches another milestone. It's the sense of urgency to pour every bit of maternal wisdom into her daughter before she leaves the nest. It's the sigh of satisfaction to see a young woman emerge who can fold fitted sheets as well as discern between a great guy and a possible felon.

But more than any of these, it's the heartwarming joy of a mother just looking at her daughter's face—that beautiful, precious face she first saw on a sonogram and has never tired of beholding. The face that inspires her to gently cup her hands around it and say, "Get that hair out of your eyes, or I'll grab some scissors and do it myself!"

Every mother knows such words come from love. Granted, they come in a roundabout, convoluted, get-some-counseling kind of way, but they do, in fact, come from love. Our daughters, however, disagree. "Love? You're nitpicking because you love me? Yeah, right."

Love is the most important thing. Even God said so. But loving people isn't always easy—especially when said people use our hair spray without asking and don't bother to put it back.

Smotherly Love is a humorous collection of conflicts between moms and daughters. You'll read about my mom, my daughter, and me—and also dozens of other moms and daughters who shared their conflicts with me in personal interviews. Enough time has passed since their clashes that both could recount the details (which don't always jibe) with humorous hindsight.

Though I'll offer advice regarding mother-daughter drama throughout this book, I need to collect it when the problem lies with me. Scripture is my first stop; then I pray and confer with my husband. If the problem persists, I run it by my godly girlfriends. After all, Proverbs 11:14 says (in my paraphrase), "Life without a sounding board of wise friends leads to disaster, but abundant feedback keeps you from going crazy or doing something stupid."

If only I'd consulted them before buying that pair of open-toed boots.

Anyway, *Smotherly Love* is far from a solve-it-all-in-one-sitting book. But as you listen to moms and daughters vent, as you smile (or gasp) when you see yourself in their stories, and as you watch them come to their senses, you'll gain insight to help everyday life go a little more smoothly with the mother or daughter you'll always love but don't always like. Together, we'll see how smotherly love can be replaced with God's perfect love in these moment-by-moment situations.

And for those women (mothers or adult daughters) I asked to interview but frowned and responded, "Why would I want to bring all that up?" I have a special message: lighten up and move on, because you're missing out.

Let the mother-daughter party begin!

"She's So Picky!"

· Chapter 1 ·

ALMONDS AT TEN PACES

Well, either side could win it,
or it could be a draw.

—*Ron Atkinson*

She Says . . .

Debi (mother)

Standing in her garden, the pioneer woman dabbed her sweaty face with her calico apron and said, "I have slaved in the hot sun. I have pulled weeds. I have toted water. My backbreaking labor has saved my family from starvation."

That's exactly how I feel when I make snack mix.

Except for the hot sun part.

And the weeds.

And the thing about toting water.

Anyway, it's not easy finding a healthful family snack that's convenient too. Thus, I created my special blend of snack mix: equal part raisins, peanuts, sunflower seeds, and carob chips. But the first time I splurged on almonds is most memorable.

Ah, what a feeling of accomplishment to view a dozen plastic storage bags of nutritious snack mix (with almonds). Keeping them on hand in all situations proved that *I am a good mother.*

Then my teenage daughter ruined the whole thing.

Driving home after an errand, I noticed Elizabeth in my rearview mirror, her face pale from having skipped breakfast. I offered her a bag of snack mix (with almonds). A few minutes later, I asked if she felt better.

"Yeah."

"And *why* do you feel better?"

Elizabeth rolled her eyes and parroted the required response with a long-suffering sigh: "Because you're a good mother who always has healthy snack mix on hand."

"That is correct," I said. "Now pass the bag back to me."

Elizabeth lobbed into my lap a nearly empty bag holding a gummy blob of raisin rejects. This forced me to break my don't-shriek-and-drive rule.

"What have you done?"

"What?"

"You ate all the almonds!"

"So?"

"The almonds were part of the snack mix! You're not supposed to pick them all out and leave what you don't like!"

"You never said I couldn't eat the almonds."

"That's because I assumed you understood snack-mix etiquette. It's a *mix*. I made it as a mix, and you are supposed to eat it as a mix."

"But I always eat snack mix that way."

My horrified gasp sucked all the oxygen out of the car. I lowered the window and shifted my mouth into overdrive.

"Elizabeth, you have betrayed my trust. Besides, I splurged on those almonds as a special treat, and you just . . . just . . . just pillaged my almonds!"

"Mom, calm down. It's not that big a deal. Sheesh."

"Don't you 'sheesh' me, young lady!"

She Says . . .

Elizabeth (daughter)

"Please? I'll give you two of my Oreos!"

This common bid for my delectable, mom-made snack mix during my high school lunch break never worked—until recently.

It all changed during a family drive with my mother behind the wheel. I sat in the backseat pouting about my rumbling tummy when my mother's brow, furrowed in concern, appeared in the rearview mirror.

"Oh, honey. You look pale. Do you need some snack mix?" Her teeth sparkled as she said this line, thinking herself to be June Cleaver offering a cure for cancer. Mom handed a bag of snack mix to me from her purse, and I began munching away in my usual custom. First, I savored the sacred almonds. Then, after getting the raisins out of the way, I ate each peanut between two carob chips. Always last were the abundant sunflower seeds.

Then my mother's palm appeared over the backseat to collect the empty bag.

Suddenly, the once-tender gaze in the mirror turned into a piercing, fiery glare.

"You ate all the almonds!" my mother shrieked.

"Yes . . ." Was this some sort of trick question? "I also ate the raisins, carob chips, and peanuts."

"As a mix?"

"No. One at a time."

"But that's . . . that's . . . *unnatural*!"

Hoping for backup, I glanced at my father, who sat strapped in the suicide seat. No luck. I was going down—but not without a fight.

"So what exactly is wrong with that?" I asked, keeping my tone calm and my words even.

"It is a *mix*! As evidenced by its name, it is to be eaten accordingly." My mom drew this out as though I were stupid. "And as if your barbaric treatment of this highly nutritious recipe wasn't bad enough, YOU ATE ALL THE ALMONDS!"

I will testify that the foundations of the earth trembled as she spoke that last phrase. But I refused to tremble before her.

"What's the problem?" I asked. "At home, there's a whole container filled with identical bags, almonds intact. Besides, it doesn't matter how I eat the stuff as long as I'm not making a mess."

But her wrath would not be abated, so the argument continued in a never-ending circle of doom until we arrived home. Dad and my brother dove for cover while we females duked it out.

I stormed into the kitchen and retrieved the container holding many more bags of precious snack mix (with almonds!) to show my enraged mother, but she could not be reasoned with.

How Would You Deactivate the Mother's Picky Button?

a. Condition Debi's picky response. Every time she complains about something inconsequential, make her listen to *Fran Drescher Sings the Blues.*

b. Give her a lifetime supply of almonds if she'll promise to shut up.

c. What picky button? Debi's not picky. She's reasonable and completely right.

Debi Says . . .

Dear Readers,

Here we go! When the problem is with me or mine, and after I've sought help from heaven and husband, I solicit advice from friends.

Giggling when I told them about the snack-mix incident, they said things like, "I'll trade you advice for a bag of snack mix!" or "How many almonds will you give me?" *Humph.* Maybe I need new friends. Or maybe I need to get over myself and just let it go. Yeah. I'll try that for a change and see what happens.

Meanwhile, here's their counsel:

- "You should loosen up. Five years from now, no one—not even you—will care how Elizabeth ate the snack mix."
- "Delegate the snack mixing to Elizabeth, and then eat her specialty however she commands."
- "Close each snack bag with a sticker that says, 'By breaking this seal you agree to all the terms and conditions of the manufacturer and will not eat the ingredients one at a time.'"
- "Next time someone threatens your almond joy, refrain from shelling them. Otherwise, this nut obsession will turn you into a fruitcake."

Don't I have great friends? I shouldn't be picky about them either.

God Says . . .

"Watch the way you talk. . . . Say only what helps, each word a gift. . . . Be gentle with one another, sensitive" (Ephesians 4:29, 32 MSG).

Help Me Say . . .

Lord, deliver me from nitpicking! I don't want to stir up discouragement and defensiveness in others. Please redirect my sensitivity from piddly details to my daughter's needs. If I must speak at all, inspire me to do so with gentleness and sensitivity. Amen.

· *Chapter 2* ·

A TENTS SITUATION

I got in an argument with [someone] inside of a tent. That's a bad place for an argument, because I tried to walk out, and had to slam the flap.

—Mitch Hedberg

She Says . . .

Ellen (mother)

My reputation as a neat freak is totally undeserved.

I don't follow my family around with sanitary wipes. I don't go ballistic if someone leaves dirty dishes in the sink. I don't vacuum obsessively to leave parallel tracks in the carpet. But it does bother me if clutter builds up for days, weeks, and possibly months.

Things really boiled over at spring break. My two oldest—Gabriel, age sixteen, and Olivia, age fourteen—can easily keep themselves occupied and out of trouble. But Alexia (who insists on being addressed as "Lou"—don't ask) is nine. She is a beautiful and delightful child who is also highly creative (translation: "not concerned about details, organization, or the passage of time").

Before I left for work on the first day of spring break, Lou asked if she could make a tent, which usually means just tacking a sheet over her bunk bed. Against my better judgment, I consented. *After all, it's spring break. I should let her do something special.*

Silly, silly me.

When I returned home, I literally could not see Lou's room. Lou, with the help of her friend Mia and sister Olivia, pillaged my linen closet for virtually every blanket, sheet, and pillow to construct a sprawling subdivision of tents in her room. Tents began at the ceiling and covered everything—furniture included—wall to wall. Peeking inside various tents, I cringed at the tumbled, chaotic clutter of clothes, books, toys, dog treats, and endless ribbons of toilet paper, courtesy of our teething puppy.

I did not scream. I did not yell. I did not explode. Surely my calm response would merit some kind of parenting award with a luxury vacation.

"Lou, you went overboard," I said, "but it's spring break. If you will clean up the mess inside the tents, you can keep them up for the rest of the week."

Days passed, and the clutter remained. On the last night of spring break, I reached my limit and declared, "There will be no more tents. There will be no more fun. *No . . . more!*"

Lou finally hustled, but she also cut corners. She took four sheets and just rolled up the tent contents, effectively creating four giant egg rolls of clutter.

So I blew up.

And there's not a jury in the land that would convict me.

She Says . . .

Lou (daughter)

I had a tent in my room.

It started off my bunk bed as usual, but then we started using push pins in the wall, and all I could think was, *Yeah, baby, it's going to be huge.*

My sister, Olivia, helped me, and so did my friend Mia. Mia spent the night because she was going to move away because her dad's a soccer player. Anyway, I couldn't sleep on top of my bunk bed because of all the stuff on it. There's a desk below it and a bookshelf that came with it, and I slept under that with a blow-up mattress. I slept there for four nights, and I got eight bug bites on my fifth night.

When my mom came home that first day, she didn't scream, but her mouth and her eyes got really big and she put her hands on her head. She said that whatever we got out, we had to put away.

My mother never says anything is organized. But in my bathroom, I have my mouthwash in the corner with my deodorant and my purple toothbrushes together. I think that's organized.

But I can't organize *everything*. There's too much stuff. Like big bags of hand-me-downs. I don't know what to do with them. And I have a lot of books on my shelves.

Some are baby books that I could get rid of, but Mom won't let me because she wants to keep all my baby stuff.

She's upset now because of the tents. I had permission, but I guess the tents got too big. Then Toby Jones, our dog, kept coming in my room and destroying it even more, so I got mad at him.

When my mom told me to pick up the stuff underneath the tents, I said, "This is going to be tough."

I sorted everything into groups, like clothes, nail polish, trash, and hair things. Some of the groups stayed in the tents, but some I stuffed behind my dresser or in my toy box.

Mom came back to check the next day and said, "Taz came through this room!" and I said, "Who's Taz?" So we looked up the Tasmanian devil from the Cartoon Network.

Then she said I procrastinate, and I said, "What's procrastinate?" She said it's when you put things off.

I'm getting really tired of all this cleaning and learning.

How Would You Deactivate the Mother's Picky Button?

a. Ellen must either eat toast that fell on the floor at breakfast or go hungry the rest of the day.

b. For one week, she must answer phone calls with, "This is Ellen. Messes are fun!"

c. Forbid her from ironing sheets and towels ever again.

Debi Says . . .

Dear Ellen,

I love tents. Some of my happiest childhood memories are of making and playing in tents. I once refused to buy a certain dining room table because its pedestal design was anti-tent. At the end of 1999, my husband bought a tent in preparation for the much-feared Y2K disaster. Not being forced to live in it is one of my life's greatest disappointments.

All that to say, I'm having a hard time toeing the maternal line on this one. But in our e-mail exchanges about this story (which happened long enough ago that you could finally think calmly about it), you came up with doable and proactive solutions:

- Define *tent* with Lou ahead of time, perhaps by approving her "blueprints."
- Set limits for appropriate tent materials.
- Agree on a deadline for tent demolition.

To your wise strategy, I would add this:

- Spend one night in the tent with her.

God Says . . .

"But you, brothers and sisters, never become tired of doing good" (2 Thessalonians 3:13 NCV).

Help Me Say . . .

Heavenly Father, nudge me. Remind me to slow down long enough to share my expectations with clarity and gentleness to my daughter. I want her to be free to play, knowing she can express herself creatively without fear of a stressful showdown at the end. These are good things that I often forget or feel too busy to do. May my instruction come from you—even instruction to play alongside my daughter sometimes. Amen.

· *Chapter 3* ·

DON'T BURST MY BUBBLE

What is elegance? Soap and water!

—Cecil Beaton

She Says . . .

Nancy (mother)

I don't ask for much.

I'm a single mom with a high-pressure job. My life is usually stressful and my house is often messy, but my bathroom—my beautiful bathroom—is my haven. It's my only oasis of order and calmness.

Coty, my only child, and I decorated it with a Monopoly theme when she was fifteen. There's a shower curtain that looks like the game board. The walls are white, the rugs are black, and the towels are in Monopoly blue, green, yellow, and red. She and I made wall decorations using pieces from a real Monopoly game.

The room is perfect.

I can walk in that bathroom and immediately feel content and at peace. It reminds me of the happy hours of playing Monopoly and the fun of transforming the bathroom from ho-hum pastels with fluffy flowers into bold colors with sharp lines.

The room *was* perfect.

More than once, I've walked in to find my haven completely destroyed: the soap was moved. There's a lip around the edge of the sink, a perfect place for the soap dispenser. It needs to stay in its designated spot to the left of the faucet, inside the lip. But time and again I discover it on the *right* side of the faucet, *outside* the lip.

"Coty, please put the soap dispenser back where it belongs after you use it."

"OK."

The next day, same thing. And the next day and the next day and the next day until finally I have to bring the hammer down.

"Coty!"

"What?"

"I love you, but would you *please* put the soap back in its proper spot?"

"It has a spot?"

"Yes, Coty. The spot where you pick it up every time, to the left of the faucet and inside the lip. That is the good spot. The spot where you set it down every time, to the right of the faucet outside the lip, is the bad spot. See? Only use the good spot."

Though she agreed, my haven was demolished the next day.

"COTY SHEREE!"

"What?"

"Quit moving the soap from its proper spot!"

"Mom, I can't help it. I'm right-handed and you're left-handed."

"So what are you saying? That I'm obsessive-compulsive?"

"No . . . and I didn't say you're paranoid either."

"Not so loud, Coty. Someone may be listening."

"Well, if they decide to wash their hands in here, they'd better put the soap back in the right place."

"What did you say?"

"Nothing, Mom. Nothing. I love you too."

She Says . . .

Coty (daughter)

My mom is the coolest. She can make *anything* fun—even going to the dentist's office. We looked at magazines together there and found a great recipe for chicken Italiano.

Not long after, we cooked it side by side in the kitchen. Mmm . . . it smelled so good! Before setting the table, I stepped into the bathroom to wash the chicken germs off my hands. (Yes, my mother has trained me well to fear all manner of microscopic menaces.)

Mom even made washing my hands fun because of our bathroom. She and I decorated it when I was fifteen with a Monopoly theme. I grabbed the soap dispenser from the left corner of the sink and squirted some into my palm. As warm, soapy water lathered my hands, warm, fuzzy thoughts filled my head about my super-cool and awesome mom. *I've got the best mom in the world. She valued my opinion when we were redecorating. She teaches me how to cook.*

After I rinsed and dried my hands, I returned to the kitchen humming a happy tune. Mom smiled at me and kissed my head as she passed by to wash her own hands.

Then it happened.

"COTY SHEREE!"

Oh no! What have I done! Had I pushed the doorknob through the wall? Left the water running? Hung the towel back crooked? It had to be both disastrous and expensive for Mom to pull the middle-name card.

I inched around the corner, and there she stood, holding the soap dispenser, smelling like chicken Italiano and anger.

"Coty, you know I love you, but . . . you didn't put the soap back. Again."

Apparently, the soap dispenser has a sacred spot on the counter. This I did not know.

I knew that the rugs had to be parallel, the towels folded precisely, and the shower curtain rings spaced evenly apart, but the soap thing was new.

After she vented, I stated my case with calm eloquence: (1) at least I washed my hands before I touched the dishes, and (2) at least I helped in the kitchen.

Five years have passed, and we live in a new house where I have my own bathroom that my mom still uses occasionally. Though we often laugh about the soap dispenser from the Monopoly bathroom, we know that we're not quite beyond the pettiness when I have to say, "Mom, you know I love you, but . . . you left the lid off the toothpaste. Again."

How Would You Deactivate the Mother's Picky Button?

a Rig the soap dispenser à la Indiana Jones so that when it's lifted from "the good spot," a steel cage will trap the offender.

b Dangle soap-on-a-rope over the middle of the sink.

c Don't wash hands. (Gotcha!)

Debi Says . . .

Dear Nancy,

If we surveyed a thousand people about this problem, not only would we discover that 98.5 percent of them refuse to participate in surveys, but 83 percent of them need to have their mouths washed out with soap.

In your crazy, chaotic life, having a set-apart place of order is important. And while I applaud you for limiting your requirements for perfection to just one room, I would like to offer my voice of experience as a recovering perfectionist who is still learning. (Remember my almond outburst in Chapter 1?)

My haven of calmness must be *inside of me*. Nobody can mess it up, move things around, or mar the beauty there. The place I'm speaking of is my faith walk with God. I can close my eyes and retreat to him as the Rock that shelters me. The Living Water that quenches me. The Bright and Morning Star that guides me.

Right now, I'm typing from my ugly thrift-store sofa that cost thirty bucks. I'm calm and satisfied because of what the Lord has done in my heart, not what I have done in my house. Hard lesson? You bet. Worth learning? Oh, yeah. Happier family? Ta-da!

Now if I could just learn to let go of almonds.

God Says . . .

"People look at the outside of a person, but the LORD looks at the heart" (1 Samuel 16:7 NCV).

Help Me Say . . .

Dear God, having one tiny spot the way I want doesn't seem like asking too much. Come to think of it, you could say the same thing—but the tiny spot you want is my heart. Take my hesitancy and my fear. Replace it with confident peace that because you're in control, it's OK that I'm not. I want to free-fall into your grace, not with a single shadow of doubt but with a singing shout of joy! And I want my daughter to fall right along with me. Help me model trust to her. Amen.

"She's So Clueless!"

· *Chapter 4* ·

QUEST FOR A DRESS

I dress up for awards, but only if somebody
else is going to pay for the clothes.
And shop for them too.

–Tea Leoni

She Says . . .

Beth (mother)

Debi is my only daughter, and I love her dearly. I remember writing on her birth announcements, "I can hardly wait to dress our little girl in pretty frills and ruffles," but that dream died years ago. Debi may be smart and beautiful, but bless her heart, she doesn't have a clue about shopping for clothes.

Because I grew up wearing mostly homemade clothes, I think it's a special treat to pick out store-bought ones. But Debi has resisted me at every turn. As a toddler, she'd throw herself on the sidewalk and pitch a fit before entering any store. She didn't like shopping any better when she was in grade school, so I'd buy clothes for her and bring them home.

"Ew!" she'd say. "These are ugly!"

"Fine. We'll take them back, and you can pick out something *you* like."

But even then, she'd turn up her finicky, freckled nose at one adorable outfit after another. I'd beg her to at least try one on: "It looks different off the hanger. You might really like it when you have it on."

When Debi finally shuffled out of the dressing room, I found it hard to believe she was a straight-A student: tags sticking out the back, buttons in the wrong buttonholes, and the waistband hiked up and twisted. "I told you it wouldn't fit," she'd pout.

"It might fit if you put it on right!" As I adjusted Debi's clothes, I also checked the quality. With my years of sewing experience, I knew the importance of stripes matching up, seams being straight, and buttons being accounted for.

"Mom, stop it! I don't like it!"

Debi wouldn't perk up to participate in dressing herself better even when a big event, such as prom, was pending. More than once, she ignored my gentle reminders about buying a formal dress until the day before prom. Of course, by then the selection was pitiful, and I had to bite my tongue to keep from saying, "If you'd gone shopping a month ago like I asked, you'd have more to choose from!"

For a long time I worried that if Debi didn't outgrow this anti-shopping, anti-dressing-nicely problem, she'd never be able to maintain a decent workplace wardrobe. I feared she would turn down good-paying, professional jobs in favor of stuffing envelopes from home—just so she could wear T-shirts and jeans every day.

Oh, no. Please tell me that's not why she became a writer.

She Says . . .

Debi (daughter)

There are a few mutant genes in our family. My mother lacks the gene for chocolate addiction. I consider this a constant source of shame. But I'm not perfect either: I'm missing the gene needed to enjoy shopping, especially for clothes, and this breaks my mother's heart.

Oh, well.

She has harped at me about my wardrobe all my life, especially during my high school years.

"Debi, all you ever wear are T-shirts and jeans."

"That's not true. I also have peasant blouses and overalls."

Besides, my T-shirts were good quality. The one that said, "It's OK, I'm with the band," was nice enough to wear with slacks. If I'd had any.

Before my junior year, my friend Janet and I drove about an hour to a bigger city with a new mall. That kind of shopping was OK because we mainly walked and talked and our moms weren't around.

I hated it when Mom dragged me to town, which was about twice a year. She forced me to try on hundreds of outfits, but they all looked the same to me: stupid. I also remember the feel of her icy-cold fingers behind my neck ("The tags need to lie flat, Debi.") and around my waist

("You've got it on sideways, Debi"). Just thinking about it makes me shiver.

Take homecoming. Or maybe it was prom. Anyway, there was a dance at school one year that I needed a long dress for. Mom kept yelling and yelling about it. And not just days ahead of time, but weeks.

"Have you thought about a dress yet?" she yelled.

"No. The dance isn't until next month."

"But we need time to shop."

"Then we'll shop next month."

"But if we wait too long, the dresses will be picked over."

"Not until next month."

Finally, the day before the dance, I gave in just to stop her harping about it.

No wonder I hated shopping for clothes. There was never anything to choose from. And every time I tried on a dress, my mother just couldn't resist doing her icy-finger inspection. She even looked at how the buttons were sewn on. I mean, who cares!

Finally, after excruciating hours spent in dozens of stores and trying every dress in my size until we found one that was tolerable, she had the nerve to ask me, "Now what about shoes?"

How Would You Deactivate the Daughter's Clueless Button?

a. Bring home a hideous dress and insist Debi wear it, thus forcing her to shop in self-defense.

b. Lure her into stores under the pretense of buying chocolate and then yank her into the dress department.

c. Give her two choices: shop early for a dress, or stay home prom night and watch professional bowling on TV with her grandmother.

Debi Says . . .

Dear Reader,

I was a doofus.

I'm still a doofus, but I can't get away with wearing a T-shirt and jeans at speaking events (unless it's a Woodstock reunion, which, by the way, I am way too young for).

Shopping should be done in short bursts sandwiched between fun stuff, like brunch and a movie. That *sounds* reasonable, but I never actually do it because shopping makes me unreasonable.

Instead, I follow this cycle:

1. Accept speaking gig with no thought about clothes because it's too far in the future.
2. As the date approaches and my assistant prompts me to get my wardrobe lined up, tell her I'm too busy.
3. Repeat step 2 over and over.
4. The day before my plane leaves, dash to the mall and be aghast at the wild new styles and popular colors.
5. Panic in the dressing room and use my cell phone to call my mother, who, without even seeing the clothes, knows instinctively what I should wear.
6. Cry in the parking lot as I realize my new outfit requires one more thing: new shoes.

God Says . . .

"If any of you need wisdom, you should ask God, and it will be given to you. God is generous and won't correct you for asking" (James 1:5 CEV).

ᘓ

Help Me Say . . .

Lord, a little help here. My daughter may be clueless about planning in advance, but I'm clueless about how far to go in helping her. Should I be more assertive and force her to participate responsibly and in a timely manner? Should I back off totally and let her experience the painful consequences of procrastination? Are there other options you can show me? Help me do whatever will help her the most. Amen.

· Chapter 5 ·

WORKING MOM GOES POSTAL

Housework can't kill you,
but why take a chance?

—Phyllis Diller

She Says . . .

Ernestine (mother)

Don't be fooled. Sleepy retirement villages in the country have plenty of drama. I know. Not only was I the pastor's wife but also the postmaster and the mother of teenage girls. Sometimes I dreamed of escaping to someplace quiet and peaceful, like inner-city New York.

As the sole employee at the post office, I worked ten hours a day—and not just sorting mail. I had to fend off a steady stream of old men who fell in love with me. One geezer gave me candy bars from his greasy pocket. Another brought a bouquet of green onions. Still another sent me flowers, letters, and gifts and asked me on a date while his wife was in the hospital. When my refusals finally penetrated his thick, bald head, he just smiled and said, "If you change your mind, you know where to find me." I had to bite my tongue to keep from replying, "Right. I'll just look for a pair of baggy overalls drenched in Old Spice."

One day the town closed because of a snowstorm, but you know the postal creed. I put in twelve long hours of mail sorting and paperwork in addition to fielding phone calls about the weather, advising how much chili powder to use in a recipe, and rejecting offers to keep old men warm.

What helped get me through was the hope of a hot meal waiting for me in a clean house. After all, my girls had two friends over to share the snow day, and certainly they'd been sweetly conspiring to surprise me. My daughter Theresa had probably cooked one of her specialties: baked chicken. Or meat loaf. Or lasagna.

At last I returned home—tired, cold, and hungry. I stepped in from the garage to the kitchen and heard three words that flipped my switch: "What's for dinner?"

Theresa had not made baked chicken. Or meat loaf. Or lasagna. All she had made was a mess.

OK, she'd had some help.

Dirty dishes covered every surface in the kitchen, the cabinet doors hung open, and the trash overflowed. Board games, clothes, pillows, soda cans, and bowls of popcorn littered the living room. In the middle of it all, the four girls sat on their lazy behinds, staring at me like clueless baby birds waiting to be fed. So I did what any normal working mother would do: I came unglued.

I turned on the dreaded Griffin Glare. This family skill, passed down from my great-great-grandma Griffin, bores holes in offspring with a single look. After I spoke with a new degree of elevation in my voice, some door slamming occurred, and I retreated to my bedroom.

Inner-city New York was looking better all the time.

She Says . . .

Theresa (daughter)

My mom loves to tell this story, and it's pretty much true. Notice I said "pretty much."

Tammy, my sister who had come home from college for a few days with a friend of hers, is really the one at fault here because she was older and should've known better. Me? I was just a sophomore in high school who hadn't left the farm yet.

Besides, Mom is missing the big picture here: snow days are not regular days. They're vacation days. Who in their right mind works on vacation? Let me think. Oh, yeah. My *mother* works on vacation.

Tammy and our friends and I hadn't spent the whole day sitting around, as my mother assumed. We cooked pancakes, eggs, and cereal for breakfast; phoned some friends and talked about boys; made soup and sandwiches for lunch; went outside to sled and make snow angels; came in and made hot chocolate and popcorn; watched TV and played cards; and then baked chocolate-chip cookies and talked about diets. Obviously, by the time my mom came home, we were just as tired as she was. Come to think of it, we were *more* tired, but she was too clueless to notice. She just shrieked, "What have you girls been doing all day?"

Always one to be helpful, I jumped in to answer first: "We played cards, and went sledding, and—"

She inhaled deeply, a sure sign she was about to lock and load the Griffin Glare.

"You girls have destroyed this house! I raised you better than this! What were you thinking?"

Note: Any question asked during engagement of the Griffin Glare is rhetorical. *Do not answer it.* That laser-like stare has been used by higher-ups in the Griffin clan for generations to let others know when they've done wrong. Estrogen-fueled Griffin women are particularly skilled at this and can, with a single look, drill to the very core of your soul.

It is not pleasant.

"You girls—and your guests—cannot have one more thing to eat or one minute of sleep until this entire house is shipshape from stem to stern!" Nautical talk from Mom is a sure sign of impending doom, so we leaped up and started cleaning while she stomped down the hallway to her bedroom.

After she slammed the door, we all agreed on two things: (1) Mom has a serious problem with overreacting, and (2) we need to move a lot faster when we hear the automatic garage door open.

How Would You Deactivate the Daughter's Clueless Button?

a Hire the school's home-economics teacher to tutor your girls privately for the entire snow day. (They'll love the personalized attention.)

b Send Theresa via overnight mail to her grandma for a more-intensive treatment with the Griffin Glare.

c Threaten to take photos of the debris and show them to prospective boyfriends.

Debi Says . . .

Dear Ernestine,

I'd send you sympathy flowers, but you'd probably assume they were from yet another adoring old man and throw them in the trash. Instead, I'm naming this outrage after you so that any working mother hence who comes home to a similar scene can say, "I've been Ernestined!"

This is a classic case of dashed expectations. Dashed, crashed, mashed, and smashed. You expected your girls to clean up after themselves and to serve you dinner. The girls expected a reprieve from the normal house rules and you to serve them dinner as usual. None of this was explicitly communicated. Hence, not only did you and your girls experience hurtful disappointment, but I got to use the word *hence* again.

To avoid a repeat, try this:

- Talk to Theresa or write her a detailed note regarding the day's expectations *before you leave for work.*
- Set an afternoon "last call" to confirm dinner plans and what needs to happen before you walk in the door.
- Order pizza if Theresa flubs dinner again . . . and make *her* pay for it.

God Says . . .

"In the morning, O LORD . . . I lay my requests before you and wait in expectation" (Psalm 5:3 NIV).

Help Me Say . . .

Dear Lord, sometimes I am so busy that my mind produces expectations faster than I can assess or communicate them. This is not a good thing. I need your help to make part of my daily routine talking strategy with you first and then my family, just like brushing my teeth or making coffee. Please empower me to do so with calmness, flexibility, and a smile! Bring unity to our family so that we work and play with equal joy and love. Amen.

· *Chapter 6* ·

SHORTCHANGED

Wal-Mart. Do they, like, make walls there?

—Paris Hilton

She Says . . .

Debi (mother)

One morning I gave Elizabeth an envelope of money for groceries at Wal-Mart. She grabbed the list from the fridge and made her fatal mistake: she *assumed* the funds would cover the items on the list. When they didn't, she had to return most of the stuff to the cashier while rehearsing the "How could you do this to me?" speech she would blast me with later.

Despite her emotional accusations (somebody give this girl a drama scholarship!), I am not to blame. Her father is.

Neal (without my knowledge) had taken the list out the day before and bought most of the items; ergo, it's his fault Elizabeth lacked funds. Why? Because he's the token male caught in a female conflict? Because he's conveniently not here to defend himself? No. Because he's a check-mark maker. When he puts an item in the shopping cart, he makes a tiny check mark by it on the list. On my lists, which Elizabeth is used to deciphering, a check mark indicates a priority item. No wonder she was confused. My original list had no check marks; but when Neal finished shopping, it had dozens of them. He also blew it by not blacking out purchased items on the list (like I do), circling the remaining items (like I do), and then losing the list on the way home (like I do).

It's good this happened, though. Experience is a memorable teacher, and Elizabeth long ago tuned out my repetitious warnings to make certain of the details, to confirm, verify, validate, confirm, double-check, make sure, confirm.

But perhaps I was too vague.

"Mom! The drugstore didn't give me the correct change! They owe me ten bucks!"

"Did you count your change before you left the checkout?"

"No."

"Tough luck, toots."

Another time she ranted about how unfair a teacher was because he didn't announce part of an assignment's requirements until the day before it was due.

"Elizabeth, did he give you a hard copy of the assignment weeks ahead of time as usual?"

"Yeah."

"Did you turn it over to see if more instructions were on the back?"

"I didn't have to! His instructions are always one-pagers!"

"Do me a favor and check anyway. I'll wait."

A minute later, Elizabeth returned, sputtering, "Well, he shouldn't put stuff on the back without a notice at the bottom to turn the page over. He is so unfair!"

Life is unfair. It's not fair that my friend Larena can eat like a truck driver and remain a thin petite. It's not fair that the literary world never valued my mermaid poetry. And it's not fair that Elizabeth blasted me for something that wasn't my fault.

She Says . . .

Elizabeth (daughter)

It happened on a beautiful April afternoon. The sun shone in a cloudless sky, a delightful breeze kissed my face, and I drove down the highway with my windows open, screaming all the way home.

That morning, Mom had given me an envelope of cash for the grocery list on the fridge. After picking up my brother, Andrew, from school, I drove to the wonderful world of Wal-Mart.

One bunch of celery. One gallon of milk. One carton of eggs. With the final few necessities in the cart, I hurried through the crowd of working mothers. That's never difficult, because their carts weigh a ton and they're distracted by their kids, cell phones, and makeover magazines.

Beep. Beep. Beep.

One by one, our items' prices flashed on the digital display. Andrew, a seasoned assistant shopper, loaded the last bag into the cart when our total lit up the screen. *How can that be right!?* I was way short.

Red-faced, we began returning things: A bag of frozen chicken. A carton of cottage cheese. A box of laundry soap. Then, from the plethora of impatient customers watching me surrender my tampons, a friendly voice called, "Elizabeth Stack! Is that you?"

Invisible. I am invisible. Poof!

But no. A family friend wanted to catch up. I kept my head down and mumbled short responses while handing back more groceries. Questions, questions, questions! Could this woman not take a hint? Did it never cross her mind to bail me out? Where's a crack in the earth when you need it?

The seething shoppers in line knew about our tight finances, since we had to put things back at Wal-Mart, so I might have accidentally, inadvertently, and completely unintentionally in a loud voice let some embarrassing medical information about my mother slip out, some of which might actually be true—but since she didn't give me enough money to buy what was on the list, it serves her right.

As Andrew and I carried the few remaining groceries to the car, my embarrassment turned to anger. And thus I drove home screaming out my car window.

How could my mother have been so clueless? She has decades more shopping experience than I do. Didn't she know the money wouldn't buy everything on the list? I trusted her, and she humiliated me in front of the entire world—because, as everybody knows, what happens at Wal-Mart does not *stay* at Wal-Mart.

How Would You Deactivate the Daughter's Clueless Button?

a Reward detail awareness in a game: "You're warm . . . getting colder . . . warmer . . . warmer . . . hot, hot, hot, yes! You noticed your hair is on fire! Here's a gummy bear."

b Put Elizabeth in therapy to *become* an obsessive-compulsive personality.

c Tattoo a disclaimer on her forehead: "Detail impaired."

Debi Says . . .

Dear Reader,

Since I'm too close to this situation to see clearly, I again sought advice from friends. The best counsel came from Christine:

> Mission control, we have lost communication. A commander never sends his troops out ill equipped and lacking in essential knowledge, and you didn't personally go over the list before handing it off to your daughter. You can't really blame a soldier . . . um . . . daughter who is trained to follow orders for not questioning the commander. You gave her a list, gave her money, and then sent her on her way. Wake up, Debi. Communication is essential for completing a mission, even if it is only at Wal-Mart.

As surprised as I was to be found at fault, I love Christine's advice. It's true. It's practical. It's wise. So why didn't I think of it? Plain and simple, I was overwhelmed by my own emotions and needed a godly friend to state the obvious. Sort of like slapping someone who's panicking, which I've always wanted to do (slap someone, that is—not panic).

God Says . . .

"Suppose one of you wants to build a tower. Will he not first sit down and estimate the cost to see if he has enough money to complete it? For if he lays the foundation and is not able to finish it, everyone who sees it will ridicule him, saying, 'This fellow began to build and was not able to finish'" (Luke 14:28–30 NIV).

Help Me Say . . .

Lord, I need your forgiveness and my daughter's too. She's not the clueless one here; I am. I didn't count the cost of being in a hurry, which led to abbreviated (and incomplete) communication. And though I get frustrated at my daughter for not confirming details, I didn't do it myself. While I'm at it, I need to seek my husband's forgiveness for blaming him. Thank you that even though owning up to my mistakes hurts at the time, it never fails to bring me closer to the ones I love—you most of all. Amen.

· *Chapter 7* ·

TEXT ME

I was dating this guy and we would spend all day text-messaging each other. And he thought that he could tell that he liked me more [than I liked him] because he actually spelt the word "YOU" and I just put the letter "U."

–Kelly Osbourne

She Says . . .

Janet (mother)

If I could name a new cell phone company, it would be "Circular." Why? Because that's the direction every conversation about cell phones goes with my sixteen-year-old daughter, Kelsey.

"Mo-om, everyone has text messaging but me!"

"That's not true. You can receive text messages."

"But what good is that if I can't reply? You and Dad have to upgrade our plan so I can text back."

"You don't need to text back. Open the text messages and then call your friends back and actually talk to them."

"That is so lame, Mom. If they wanted to talk to me, they'd call me."

"Bingo, Kelsey. That's why we have cell phones. So we can talk, not text."

"But if I open the text messages to see who called and what they want, you and Dad complain about having to pay for them. If you guys would upgrade our plan, it would save money in the long run, and the whole family could text as much as they wanted."

"Kelsey, you're the only one who wants to text."

"No, I'm not. Tyler wants to text."

"Your brother doesn't even have a cell phone."

"But he needs one for high school, just like I do. With the plan you and Dad have now, you're paying up to eight bucks a month for limited texting, right?"

"Right."

"Then why not pay just a couple bucks more so everyone can have unlimited texting?"

"Why not *save* about eight bucks a month by not doing any texting?"

"Mo-om!"

"Kelsey, I don't understand. You can talk a lot faster than you can text."

"But why risk going over in minutes if you can text for free?"

See what I mean? Around and around we go.

Her dad and I eventually gave in after Kelsey, with the assistance of her brother and her friend Sierra, made a compelling case with detailed comparisons among several plans. But that's not what won me over. My phone—my wonderful, nonflip, basic blue phone that merely does calls and texts—was *free*.

My bubble of bliss popped, though, when I received this text message from Kelsey: "Chk out Zing-Mobile plan. Free camera fonz w/ MP3!"

She Says . . .

Kelsey (daughter)

I'm worried about my parents.

They handle all the adult stuff like work and bills and taxes, which kind of surprises me because they don't seem to understand numbers very well—especially the numbers in cell phone plans.

"Mom, I'll say it again: paying for each text message one at a time is more expensive than upgrading to a plan that lets everyone in our family do unlimited texting."

"But, Kelsey, you're the only one who wants to text."

"That's because I'm the only one who knows how. You and Dad would text all the time if you tried it."

"I don't think so. My cell phone is just for emergencies."

"Right. Next time you're on a sinking ship and they need to toss the really heavy stuff overboard, give them your phone."

"Kelsey!"

"Mom, your phone is huge! It looks like you're listening to one of Dad's slippers."

"Upgrading is too expensive."

"Mom, if you upgrade, your phone is free."

"Free?"

That got her attention. But where I look at a free phone as the point of departure for adding extra features, Mom just accepts the free phone. Hers is boring blue and doesn't even flip. But my phone, on which I got a great deal online, is hot pink with glittery silver stars, flips, and can take pictures. I taught her and Dad how to do texting, and my older brother, Tyler, who's also in high school, texts all the time too.

But Mom still doesn't understand the numbers.

"Kelsey, our upgrade to include texting started in the middle of the month, and you had 3,800 messages."

"No, I didn't."

"Yes, you did."

"Let's see how many I have on my phone right now: 947."

"And today's only the eighth!"

"But the month started on the twenty-seventh."

"Kelsey, the month starts on the first. All months do."

See what I mean? She just doesn't get it.

Now the cell phone bill is a family joke. My dad waits to open it until we're all at the dinner table. We say whoever did the most texting is the most popular, and then we tease whoever did the least. Last month's bill was typical. My text messages: 3,990; Tyler's: 1,799; Mom's: 151; Dad's: 54.

What's even sadder is that Dad always sends more than he receives. That's gotta hurt, but I'm going to make him feel better by texting him a couple hundred times before next month.

Sigh . . . contributing to the family makes me feel so good!

How Would You Deactivate the Mother's Clueless Button?

a Show Janet the math *again*. Paying five cents for each of the family's 5,994 messages in one month would equal $299.70, versus $9.95 a month for unlimited texting.

b Petition the government to require people over age forty to read *Cell Phones for Dummies*.

c Create a support group for textaphobics with Kelsey's parents as charter members.

Debi Says . . .

Dear Janet,

Give it up.

You and I have been dethroned as authorities on technology. Our kids considered us all-powerful when they were little because we could change the bulb in their nightlights. Now we come to them for technical advice on life-or-death emergencies like downloading missed episodes of *Lost*.

Text-messaging is the new national pastime, so don't freak when Kelsey gets thousands of messages. She is not a drug dealer. She is a typical teenager with lots of friends who also coerced their parents into buying unlimited texting plans. (Although, as you told me, you are proud of Kelsey for finding a good deal for your family.)

Many teenagers may claim they're not addicted to text-messaging, but don't fall for it. I recently spotted a couple of girls with their heads bowed in public. They weren't praying but texting. To each other.

To keep Kelsey from reaching that point, try this:

- Have a family charging station so that cell phones are not within her reach between 10:00 p.m. and 7:00 a.m.
- Make her take piano lessons so all her fingers stay as buff as her texting thumbs.
- Limit the number of daily texts to not exceed the number of flip-flops she owns. (This may require buying more flip-flops.)

God Says . . .

"Do your best to improve your faith. You can do this by adding goodness, understanding, self-control, patience, devotion to God, concern for others, and love" (2 Peter 1:5–7 CEV).

Help Me Say . . .

Lord, the time when I had all the answers as a mom is past. Thank you for my sharp (and persistent!) daughter to point out where I lack understanding. But thank you also for the honor you've given me of nurturing her faith walk: in patience, in self-control, in love. By your unlimited grace, may the way I live draw her closer to you. Amen.

"She's So Stubborn!"

· *Chapter 8* ·

SLEEPING BEAUTY AND THE BEAST

I love sleep. My life has the tendency to fall apart when I'm awake, you know?

—Ernest Hemingway

She Says . . .

Debi (mother)

In Elizabeth's toddler days, she awoke with each sunrise, padded into my bedroom, and called, "Mor-ring! Happy day!" If I didn't budge, she'd reach under the blanket and pull on my ankles. "Feet on floor, Mama! Feet on floor!"

Oh, how the mattress has flipped.

She's pushing twenty now, and I'm the one who tries to wake her—often at two in the afternoon.

"Elizabeth."

Silence.

"Elizabeth!"

Silence.

"LIZ!"

"Unn."

"Sweetheart, you're sleeping the day away. You need to get up."

"Unn."

"Remember how you told me last night that you were going to put in job applications today? You also need to run errands before picking up your brother from school."

"Unn."

Her monosyllabic "unn" is equivalent to a single character of hieroglyphics that represents dozens of words. Allow me to translate for you.

- *First unn*: "I'm acknowledging your harping voice only to make you stop repeating my name and get to the point of why you're hassling me."
- *Second unn*: "As much as I would like to sleep the day away, I can't because your every interruption requires me to start my sleep cycle over again. So save us both a lot of time and just go away."
- *Third unn*: "I've completely tuned you out because you always say the same thing, which makes me want to escape to my fantastic dream world where I am Lara Croft defusing a bomb, kicking bad guys' butts, and negotiating with a crazed black-market arms dealer who bears an eerie resemblance to you."

I never believed Elizabeth's claims that her bed holds her captive until recently.

Trying to rouse her at noon, I fell for her lie-down-with-me-and-talk-me-awake ploy. Her enveloping mattress, downy pillows, and cuddly blankets created a womblike atmosphere. The traffic outside her window lulled us both to the brink of sleep, and the cats snuggling up to doze pushed us over the edge. When I awoke, the clock read four in the afternoon. Her bed is now taboo.

What irks me most, though, is Elizabeth's rationalization of her snooze-a-thons by pointing out the few times I slept in because of piddly things like childbirth, deadlines, or major surgery.

The point is, it's OK when I sleep in, but not when Elizabeth does.

She Says . . .

Elizabeth (daughter)

I love my bed.

It's full-sized on a white antique frame with six standard pillows and one body pillow. I have a sheet, down quilt, knitted blanket, and comforter to swaddle me.

I am also a heavy sleeper.

Tornadoes, thunderstorms, and fire trucks can pass through at night without disturbing me. So to awake each morning, three alarms sound at intervals starting two hours before my desired time of consciousness.

First, my iPod has a "Wake Me Up!" playlist that starts with Irish folk tunes and gradually amplifies to "Alive" by P.O.D.

Second, my cell phone's alarm tricks my subconscious into thinking I have a call. (But it doesn't wake me up because "in my sleep" I set it to vibrate. Heh, heh.)

Third, my pocket-sized alarm goes off at fifteen, ten, and then five minutes with a shrill wailing sound like a yak in labor with triplets.

However, due to my vivid imagination and exciting dream life, my mind thwarts these electronic endeavors by telling me that I, Lara Croft, need to deactivate the "bomb" to complete my mission (which is to sleep for as long as possible).

Naturally a light sleeper, Mom hears my alarms as they

begin sounding at 5:00 a.m. Even though she has slept into the afternoon on many occasions (such as days of the week ending in *y*), she is perturbed with me. Then, when I do not emerge until nearly noon, she is exasperated.

Picture her standing in my doorway, clad in a coarse dress and a plaid hair kerchief with her chin sprouting two disturbingly long hairs. Her thick accent (impeded by her lack of teeth) nags into my brain.

"Get up out of ze bed! Scrub ze floors! Feed ze pigs! Get ze college degree and zen be getting married! Ven vill you make ze grandchildren before I must die! And also for me make ze famous brownies from ze secret recipe! Get hup! Now!"

And Mom has the audacity to wonder why I don't emerge from my cavern of security and sweet silence each morning with the singing of the birds.

Don't get me wrong. I'm glad to help out. I'm getting free rent in exchange for my pleasant and rather helpful assistance. But a girl needs her beauty sleep.

Now if you'll excuse me, I need some quality time with my pillow.

How Would You Deactivate the Daughter's Stubborn Button?

a Install a taxi cab meter in Elizabeth's room that runs up her "fare" during sleep: $2.99 for the first hour and a dollar for every hour after that equals at least $9.99 a day. Times that amount by 365 days in a year for a total of $3,646.35—guess who's going on a cruise!

b Remove Elizabeth's bed and make her sleep dangling from a hook over whichever is scariest: a pit of crocodiles, a tank of piranhas, or a group of nine-year-old boys who just learned the words to "Beans, beans, the magical fruit . . ."

c When all else fails, try dynamite.

Debi Says . . .

Dear Reader,

Elizabeth put the "rrrr" in "strrrrong willed," aging her dad and me before our time. We've prayed, talked, acted, pleaded, disciplined, rewarded, and even sought professional help in parenting this delightful but challenging girl.

My friends didn't know the struggle we were having with her in this area until now. Here's a glimpse at their advice:

- "Let Elizabeth choose two days each week to sleep in, but for the other five she must go to bed early *and* get up early."
- "Box up her bed and replace it with an army cot."
- "If she's not a full-time employee or a full-time student with a 3.0 GPA, make her pay rent or move out."
- "Lara Croft didn't get to be the tomb raider by sleeping like she was dead. Unless you're the boss or work the night shift, snoozing till noon is the opiate of the unemployed. Boot your daughter out of bed at dawn and inform her of her new mission: to actively pursue, secure, and maintain a job. This advice will self-destruct in five seconds."

God Says . . .

"It is never fun to be corrected. In fact, at the time it is always painful. But if we learn to obey by being corrected, we will do right and live at peace" (Hebrews 12:11 CEV).

Help Me Say . . .

Lord, you know I'm not experienced at parenting a young adult. Yelling, yes. Procrastinating, yes. But not setting relational boundaries—especially with constructive action and follow-through. Thanks for wise friends to point out my blind spots. Please prepare my daughter's heart and mine for this discussion. I need your grace and your guidance as I let go of her and latch on to you more than ever. Amen.

· *Chapter 9* ·

ARGUING TOOTH AND NAIL

I argue very well. Ask any of my remaining friends. I can win an argument on any topic, against any opponent. People know this, and steer clear of me at parties. Often, as a sign of their great respect, they don't even invite me.

—Dave Barry

She Says . . .

Tracie (mother)

Cassie, who is seventeen, argues with me about everything.

It's way beyond me saying black and her saying white. It's me telling her we're totally out of milk and her pointing to three sour teaspoons of milk left in the gallon jug teetering on top of the trash can. It's me warning her about frigid winter weather and her plodding through snowdrifts in flip-flops. Even with undeniable evidence to the contrary and a dozen eyewitnesses, she will not back down. Ever. It's like she's part of the Flat Earth Society.

The other day I asked her to cook dinner and have it ready at five o'clock so the family could get to our obligations that evening. When I came home, I pointed out to her that the family was hungry, no food was ready, and it was five thirty.

"No, it's not," she said. "It's 5:31."

"Fine," I said. "Then you're not just thirty minutes late with dinner, but thirty-*one* minutes late."

"Not really. The clock in my room is five minutes fast."

"So the clock in your room says 5:36?"

"Yes."

"Cassie, you're not helping yourself here. That means you're an extra *six* minutes late with getting dinner on the table."

"I am not!"

See? It makes no sense. I love Cassie with all my heart and always will, but she is the most stubborn, argumentative person I know.

The "classic Cassie" story happened recently in the car. As I drove, she sat beside me and began to bite her nails—a habit she wants to break. Not wanting to nag her, I reached over, took her hand, and held it in her lap. Not one to give in, she brought *both* our hands up to her mouth and resumed chewing on her nail. Again, not saying a word, I brought both our hands into *my* lap.

Do you know what that girl did? She is so stubborn that she leaned over to chew on her nail *while it was in my lap*, hitting her head on the steering wheel in the process! I yanked my hand free of hers to grip the wheel better and, I'm not ashamed to say this, raised my voice.

"Cassie! What are you doing?"

"I have a rough spot on my nail."

"But we could've had an accident! Your head hit the steering wheel!"

"No, it didn't."

"It did too! Didn't you feel us swerve, hear other drivers honking at us, and notice me yanking the steering wheel back to keep us on the road?"

"My head never hit the steering wheel."

"Yes, it did."

"Did not."

"Did too."

"Did not! I don't even *have* a head!"

What?

I've heard of not having a leg to stand on in an argument, but not having a head?

She Says . . .

Cassie (daughter)

Mom and I share a serious stubborn streak, which is kind of funny since she isn't my birth mom. We argue about stupid things (like school and finding my first job), but we also argue about really important stuff (like music and clothes).

I'm homeschooled, and Mom works part time. Sometimes she asks me to do some housework during the day *and* get my studies done by the time she comes home. That's impossible. I need time to chat online with my friends (social studies), watch DVDs (literature in cinema), and take a bubble bath (health and hygiene). Mom *claims* she wants me to be a well-rounded adult, but then she won't accept those things as valid educational units.

Mom also nags me about overlooking details, but I pay plenty of attention to *important* details. How else could I maintain my winning streak in *Lord of the Rings* trivia?

To Mom, though, "important details" means having dinner ready at five o'clock. I forgot once. Mrs. Details herself told me it was five thirty, but the clock actually said five-three-*one*, not five-three-*zero*. When I pointed that out, she got mad. Does she want me to notice details or not? She makes no sense and then gets mad when I use logic. To hear her tell it, if I'm speaking, I'm also arguing. This is totally untrue and could be proved in a formal debate.

Mom's favorite story about me arguing happened in the car. I was biting my nails. I mean, they're my nails, right? I wasn't biting *her* nails. Anyway, Mom didn't want me to bite them, so she held my hand, but that didn't stop me. Then she pulled our hands away from my mouth and put them both in her lap. The rough spot on the nail that was really bothering me just needed a couple more nibbles to be gone, so I leaned over. It's not that big of a deal. So what if my head hit the steering wheel? The guardrail was right there. What's there to be upset about?

Finally, Mom did something decent that I couldn't argue with her about: she gave me extra English credit.

For debate.

How Would You Deactivate the Daughter's Stubborn Button?

a. Implement a vow of silence for Cassie that expires when she moves out on her own.

b. Rent her mouth to underdeveloped countries as a power generator.

c. Agree with everything Cassie says. It will mess with her mind.

Debi Says . . .

Dear Tracie,

You are right, and I am wrong.

Not really, but I figured you've never heard those words before and might like to see them in print.

Cassie's argumentativeness reminds me of a superhero's quandary: "This power can be used for good or for evil" (as opposed to a superhero's *laundry*, which cannot be tumbled dry even though the tags say so). Why does she think every hill is worth dying on? Maybe she's afraid that being on anyone's side besides her own diminishes who she is. If so, she's got to be lonely too.

You're a smart, professional woman, Tracie. I bet you've already tried the following:

- assuring Cassie of your unconditional love;
- memorizing Bible verses together about stubbornness; and
- listing three issues each week that she will commit not to argue about.

My final advice? Designate some "argument-free zones" you can enjoy with Cassie regularly, whether it's a cozy spot to share at home or a time frame for chatting away from home.

And no argument.

God Says . . .

"Wisdom is supreme; therefore get wisdom. Though it cost all you have, get understanding" (Proverbs 4:7 NIV).

Help Me Say . . .

God in heaven, we need help. Daily arguments are obscuring the love my daughter and I share. Confirm in our hearts that winning is not the most important thing, but wisdom is—wisdom that comes from walking with you. Show me how to guide my daughter into mature discernment of when to take a stand and when to let it slide. Amen.

LOST

We're not lost. We're locationally challenged.

—John Ford

She Says . . .

Terry (mother)

A child's desire to learn can warm your heart.

It can also melt your brain.

My daughter Alexis, who's eight, nearly fried my neurons on a recent road trip in Missouri. As usual, she sat in the back with her siblings, listening to books on tape and coloring in activity books. Also as usual, I read aloud to my husband, Dave, as he drove. Then Alexis asked me a simple question that morphed our pleasure trip into a panic attack: "Where are we?"

"We're between Concordia and Higginsville."

"That's not what I mean," she said. "Where are we?"

"We're on I-70 headed west."

"No, Mom. *Where are we?*"

Dave and I exchanged looks and peered at the other kids. Were they playing a prank?

"Alexis," I said, "we're in the minivan on I-70 going west toward our home. We just passed Concordia and are almost to the Higginsville exit."

"You don't get it, Mom. I want to know where we are."

Apparently we were in the twilight zone because I heard my daughter in English and answered her in English, but we still didn't understand each other. Dave stopped at the next service station to buy a road atlas. And antacids. And aspirin.

"See, Alexis?" My finger traced our route on the new map. "We're at this spot." Dave and I thought we could return to our book in peace, but Alexis still didn't understand. Either that or she wasn't satisfied that some of my brain cells were still intact. We needed insight from a higher authority: the service station clerk.

"Excuse me," I said. "Can you tell me precisely where we are right this second?"

"Uh . . . you're here."

"Right, but how would you describe 'here'?"

"Off the highway between Concordia and Higginsville."

"Yes, but where exactly?"

When he stared at me the way I had stared at Alexis, I knew her "lost-itis" was contagious and hustled her back into the minivan. How could I explain where we were?

"We're about an hour from home."

"No, Mom. Where are we *now*?"

"We just passed exit 52."

"Mom, that isn't it. Where *are* we?"

"We're in Lafayette County."

"You missed the point, Mom. *Where are we?*"

"On the brink of insanity."

"Mo-om!"

"Two hours from the nearest mental-health facility."

"Mo-om! Stop!"

"An hour and a half from a really good orphanage."

At that point, I realized our minivan's first-aid kit and spare tire were useless. What we really needed was a Global Positioning System and a roll of duct tape.

She Says . . .

Alexis (daughter)

Our family has a rule in the minivan: anyone who asks, "Are we there yet?" has to pay a quarter. It's not fair to us kids, but our parents like it.

So on this road trip I'd been plotting how to say it a different way without having to pay a quarter. From my window I saw nothing but fields and farmhouses, which made me quit thinking about the quarter and start wondering *really* where we were. So I asked.

"We're between Concordia and Higginsville," Mom said without looking up from her book. She and Dad always take turns reading out loud and driving on trips. But because she hadn't answered my question, I asked again. She told me the highway number, but that's not what I wanted to know, so I asked again. And again. And again. She said something different every time without actually answering me. Was she playing some sort of prank?

It seemed like such a simple question. How could she not understand? I decided to keep asking until she did. Not long after that she gave Dad her "Help me!" look, and they pulled over and bought a map while we kids got drinks and snacks. (My little brother, Dawson, gave me a thumbs-up.)

"See, Alexis?" Mom said. Back in the minivan, she

unfolded the map and pointed at hundreds of different colored lines. Yeah, like that helps. She practically forced me to ask one more time: "Where are we?"

Mom made this big sigh that she only does at home when she hopes we'll say, "Never mind," to whatever is stressing her out, but I refused to give up. So the whole family got out of the minivan and walked in the gas station a second time.

Mom asked the clerk, "Where are we?"

He was a teenager and looked at us like, "Are you guys joking? I don't know. Aren't you adults supposed to know this kind of stuff?" That's not what he said, but I could tell that's what he thought, and I totally agreed with him.

The whole way home, I kept asking and Mom kept saying things but not really answering my simple, simple question: *"Where are we?"* She raised her voice a couple of times, and even Dad got snappy once, but they didn't understand.

All I wanted to know was the address to put on the envelope if I ever wanted to send a letter to one of those farmhouses I saw.

How Would You Deactivate the Daughter's Stubborn Button?

a Charge a dollar for every question that can't be answered yes or no.

b Hand Alexis the cell phone to start polling her grandparents for an answer.

c Impose a code of silence for future road trips.

Debi Says . . .

Dear Terry,

This reminds me of a wise Chinese saying: "Only a duck can measure the riverbank."

Actually, I just made that up. My husband is watching *Seven Samurai* next to me on the sofa as I type, so fortune-cookie phrasing makes *anything* sound profound right now.

Where were we? Oh, wait. You don't like that question.

When I talked with you and Alexis, four years had passed since this event. On the upside, think of how the miles flew as you and Alexis volleyed back and forth: "No, *you* missed the point!" "No, *you* missed the point!" "No, *you* missed the point!" And so on.

If something like this happens again, consider these tips:

- Ask your daughter *why* she wants to know (and forbid her from saying, "Because!").
- Tell her to write it down, and list other places she could look for the answer (library, Internet, etc.) when she gets home.
- Direct Alexis toward a career as a prosecuting attorney.

God Says . . .

"Keep on asking, and you will be given what you ask for. Keep on looking, and you will find. Keep on knocking, and the door will be opened" (Matthew 7:7 NLT).

Help Me Say . . .

Lord, I need your grace to deal with my persistent daughter! She hasn't disobeyed or rebelled, but her exceptionally inquisitive and tenacious nature challenges me daily. Please prevent me from getting frustrated with these traits that can, with your guidance, be admirable assets in her adult life. What a powerful woman of prayer she can be! Or an unstoppable defender of what's right. But I would like to live long enough to see it happen, so please give me patience and wisdom in the meantime. Amen.

"She's So Bossy!"

She Says . . .

Debi (mother)

My daughter, Elizabeth, doesn't appreciate how hard previous generations of women in our family worked.

Great-Grandma Beulah, at age eight, rose before the sun to bake bread for her family of thirteen and all the hired hands. Grandma Ione, at age ten, cleaned their farmhouse by herself every week and scrubbed floors on her hands and knees.

Me? When I was in grade school, I had to keep my room clean by regularly stashing its clutter behind boxes in the attic, thus proving that each generation of American women works harder than the one before.

Yet Elizabeth views household chores as a violation of the Diva Convention, which established that no teenage daughter must do anything she's not in the mood for.

"Maturity means you *do your job*, whether or not you feel like it," I tell her. (That's a direct quote from the Sleeva Convention, which established that mothers are required to teach their daughters how to roll up their sleeves and apply elbow grease.)

"But, Mom, I have plans today!"

"Then stop whining and start cleaning."

"But the bathrooms are disgusting!"

· *Chapter 11* ·

BATHROOM BLITZ

I hate housework. You make the beds, you wash the dishes, and six months later you have to start all over again.

—*Joan Rivers*

“If you’d clean them more often, it wouldn’t be such a big deal.”

“But I’m not the one who messed them up!”

“If you say ‘but’ one more time, I’m gonna give yours a good whack. Now do your job so we can all go on with our lives.”

At this point, Elizabeth stomps off to start scrubbing with her patented “Little Miss Shortcut” method. She claims that the smell of cleaning products makes her sick. Right. Sick of *cleaning*. Her shortcut is to use a watered-down substitute that doesn’t remove soap scum from the tile or get the toothpaste splatters off the mirror.

That’s not clean in my book.

Come to think of it, that didn’t qualify as clean in my mother’s book either when she taught me how to scrub a bathroom within an inch of its life. But I’m reformed. Year by year, I’ve lowered my household hygiene standard like a limbo stick, and now it’s so low only a Barbie convertible could clear it.

Yet when I point out to Elizabeth that the trash is still full or the soap dish is still gloppy or the tub is still icky, she gives me her “You’re a bossy tyrant” glare. It doesn’t faze me. Give her fifteen years or so, and she’ll be calling me to say, “Your granddaughter doesn’t clean correctly and then accuses me of being bossy!”

Just like I did to my mom.

She Says . . .

Elizabeth (daughter)

Goggles and face mask? Check.

Yellow rubber gloves that leave a smelly white residue on my hands? Check.

Power sander for soap scum? Check.

When Mom wrote her first book, I started doing most of the housework. Unfortunately, that included the bathrooms. I must have gone through five hundred rolls of paper towels since then, but according to Mom it should've been five thousand, because the bathroom is never clean enough. I believe that once—*once!*—after her white-gloved inspection she offered her hand in congratulations. She wants the bathrooms cleaned very specifically, with lots of bleach and elbow grease, because otherwise "they are not actually clean."

The cleaning fumes make me light-headed. They also leave me smelling like a chemical potluck. My choice of orange cleaner works better and has a pleasant scent.

There's another reason for hating bathroom duty: we have elves. Messy, mischievous elves who like to destroy all my hard work.

Picture this: I am dressed in Cinderella-like rags, kneeling on the floor with my bucket and my scrub brush. I push myself up from the glistening floor and dab perspiration from my brow. My sigh is a mixture of exhaustion and satisfaction.

Then the elves come to prance around my sparkling bathroom and wreak mayhem.

First, there is the toothpaste elf. In his dental hygiene wake are trails of gooey mintyness. How he gets it all over the sink, on the counter, and even on the toilet is beyond me.

Second is the wet-towel elf. After creating quarts of condensation to streak the mirror and moisten the walls, he leaves sopping wet towels on the floor and counter.

Finally, there is the hair elf. She dances about the bathroom singing lame '70s songs as she blow-dries and styles her hair. Strands litter the once-sparkling linoleum like flaws in a diamond. As she twirls about, she scolds, "I told you to clean the bathroom, Elizabeth, but you didn't do a thorough job. Look at all the toothpaste globs, wet towels, and hair you missed."

"You . . . you . . . you people are the ones who leave messes! It was wondrously clean just moments ago! All this hair is yours!"

"No, it's not. My hair is not that long, and it's not that color."

Even after I get the DNA results back from the lab showing a perfect match, Mom (I mean the hair elf) still refuses to acknowledge the indisputable evidence that I am the victim here.

How Would You Deactivate the Mother's Bossy Button?

a Buy a hazmat suit to make a statement.

b Sprinkle mothballs under Debi's bed to exact odiferous revenge (moowahahaha!).

c Leave the elves to fend for themselves.

Debi Says . . .

Dear Reader,

You may notice a trend in the advice my friends give me. Besides their demands to discuss my problems over cheesecake, they tend to side with my daughter! Sort of reminds me of Proverbs 27:6, which says (in my paraphrase), "Authentic friends give you the painful truth with one hand, followed by a sincere hug with both arms."

Here's what they said this time:

- "Make a list of what you want that darling of yours to clean, but have someone else inspect her work."
- "Set expectations and a schedule in writing. Household duties must be completed before the fun begins."
- "Tell Elizabeth she needs to 'work as unto the Lord'! You never know who may need to visit your powder room. An angel perhaps?"
- "Elizabeth has a valid complaint about the hazardous vapors. Get rid of the bleach and use natural products."
- "Regarding those elves, I don't know what to tell you, because I've got a couple of those creeping around my house too. Very annoying and impossible to catch!"

God Says . . .

"Finally, all of you, live in harmony with one another; be sympathetic, love as brothers, be compassionate and humble. Do not repay evil with evil or insult with insult, but with blessing" (1 Peter 3:8–9 NIV).

Help Me Say . . .

Dear God, I hate these pointless and stressful ruts of conversation my daughter and I get into sometimes! Without your help, we're doomed to disharmony. Too often we want to chastise the other but have compassion for ourselves, when it should be the other way around. Please calm our minds and keep our hearts soft toward one another. Amen.

· Chapter 12 ·

A HAIR TRIGGER

She looks like she combs her hair
with an egg beater.

—Hedda Hopper

She Says . . .

Sheri (mother)

Brittany and I have had hair issues from day one.

What really gets to me is how Brittany, who is only eleven and has wavy hair, is now bossing *me* around about how to do hair! *Me.* I have long, thick, curly hair—the most difficult kind of hair to work with. So I know—*I know*—how to take care of curly hair. But Brittany doesn't listen to me, and then every morning we go through the same routine where I'm in the bathroom getting ready for the day and she's starts whining at me through the door.

"Mo-om! Do my hair!"

"Brittany, you're old enough to do your own hair."

"Please, Mom!"

"But you always complain when I do your hair."

"Mom, just do my hair!"

"I can't. I'm putting on my makeup."

"You don't need makeup! And I *really* need my hair done!"

So I start doing her hair, which means combing it out and making sure her part isn't crooked. But as soon as I start combing, Brittany begins yelling.

"Ow! You're hurting me!"

"Did you comb out your hair last night after your shower?"

"Ow! No! I forgot!"

“Brittany, we have the same kind of hair. We have to comb it out with detangler the night before.”

“Ow! Stop pulling so hard!”

“I’ve told you this a hundred times! Now you have a rat in your hair the size of a softball.”

“I do not! Ow!”

“Actually, you have a whole colony of rats making a nest . . .”

“Ow! Mom! Quit hurting me!”

“. . . and your rat’s nest is full of rat babies . . .”

“Ow! Stop it!”

“. . . and then their rat cousins came over . . .”

“Mom!”

“. . . and they invited their rat friends . . .”

“Stop it! Ow!”

“. . . and they’re all saying, ‘Woo-hoo! It’s party time!’ ”

“It’s not funny! Ow! Ow!”

What is her problem? Brittany doesn’t do her share of caring for her hair the night before, then she bosses me in the morning. She tells me to part her hair, then she says she hates it. She tells me to make it smooth, then she says not to use gel. When she goes to ballet practice, she needs her hair in a severe bun with no wispies, which means a ton of bobby pins, and the whole time she’s saying, “Ow! The pins hurt! Ow! Put more in! Ow!”

What’s the answer? Shave her head? Give her dreadlocks? I don’t know. But wrangling with her hair is keeping us both in knots.

She Says . . .

Brittany (daughter)

My hair is dark brown and wavy with a little bit of gold and it goes down to the middle of my back. In the summer, I get highlights from the sun. Every morning, I get stressed out from my mom. (Hint to Mom: STOP IT.)

I've been trying to do my hair myself for about a year now, since the end of fourth grade. So I'm practically a pro, but my mom still does it better than me. (Hey, I said *practically*.) What I want is for my hair to be smooth with no bumps, but my mom goops in this slimy gel that stinks and then combs it through so hard it hurts. (Again, hint to Mom: STOP IT!)

Mom also has bossy rules for doing my hair at night that are hard to remember. After I shampoo and condition my hair, she wants me to comb it out with detangler. While it's drying, I can watch TV. Then she wants me to comb it out *again* (oh joy) and put it up in a twisty clip to sleep in. Who can sleep with pointy things poking your head all night? Usually I forget the rules because of my homework, ballet practice, sports, and chores. (Are you listening, Mom? LOOSEN UP!)

Mom doing my hair in the morning isn't bad if she got a lot of sleep the night before. Then she's happy and doesn't comb so hard. She'll even say, "Oh, Brittany, honey,

I didn't mean to pull your hair." But if she didn't get enough sleep, she'll be grouchy and comb it too fast and extra hard and order me around: "Hold still!" "Hand me a clip!" "You should've combed it out last night like I told you!" (All that's missing is, "And your little dog too!")

She likes to makes jokes about rats in my hair having rat babies and rat cousins. She's laughing when she says them, but it was only funny the first time. (Hint to Mom: GET NEW JOKES! But don't stay up late looking for them, because you know what happens when you don't get enough sleep.)

How Would You Deactivate the Daughter's Bossy Button?

a Divert Brittany's allowance for daily hair house calls by an independent stylist.

b Give her cornrows. (True classics never die.)

c Make her punishment be ten lashes with a wet scrunchie.

Debi Says . . .

Dear Sheri,

When I was a girl, my mother and I had identical arguments. Except the issue was who got to stay up the latest at night. And it wasn't my mom; it was my brother. So I know exactly how you feel.

Remember when we talked, you voiced a great solution: withhold Brittany's TV privileges each night until she has completed the proper hair care. See? You already knew what to do, just like Proverbs 20:5 says (in my paraphrase): "A mother's instinct is sometimes buried beneath frustration and anxiety, but talking with a friend over iced raspberry mochas will often bring wisdom to the surface."

When Brittany complains that you're bossing her, reply, "No, I'm coaching you." Then use a coaching approach in your words and actions: stay calm, keep your remarks positive, go through a few reps with her until she has the task mastered, and then pour on the praise.

If Brittany bosses *you*, stare at her until she stops. Then say, "Let's rewind this conversation so you can speak to me with respect. I really want to hear what you have to say, but your words toward me cannot be bossy."

Let me know if this works, because I'm either really good or under the influence of a *Dr. Phil* marathon.

God Says . . .

"Unless you are faithful in small matters, you won't be faithful in large ones. . . . Each one should carry his own load" (Luke 16:10 NLT; Galatians 6:5 NIV).

Help Me Say . . .

Dear God, this is tricky. In one sense, I want my daughter to grow into an independent adult who can take care of herself. In another sense, I never want her to lose childlike dependency on you for everything: small stuff now like remembering to brush her hair and big stuff later like running her own business. I can't make her find that balance, but by your grace I can model it. Show me how. Amen.

· *Chapter 13* ·

THE PROBLEM WITH PROM

Greater love hath no mom than to
prepare her daughter for prom.

—*Debi Stack*

She Says . . .

Diana (mother)

At prom time, hope didn't spring eternal; it sprang leaks.

Every year I told myself, *It doesn't have to be like last time.* Allison and I could have fun! And smile! And bond! Yet for every doo-dah one of these formal events, we sloshed around ankle deep in hysterics, hormones, and hemlines.

The learning curve for Allison's first formal nearly derailed us both at the hair salon that afternoon. The newly hired stylist created an updo on Allison's head that looked like a reject from the Tacky Wig Factory . . . that had been run over . . . then electrified.

Because Allison forgot to wear a button-up shirt to the salon, the task of removing her T-shirt over the bulbous mass of backcombing fell to me.

"Mom! Be careful! Don't make my hair worse than it already is!"

"Honey, that's not possible."

"*Mo-om!*"

Our only recourse was to start over with the hair. As I brushed out springy curls to create a smooth French roll, Allison vowed that next time she'd use a proven stylist and wear a button-up shirt. If only avoiding other perils of prom were so easy—especially Allison's metamorphosis into a corsage-wearing control freak. She barked orders at me like a platoon leader taking a hill in enemy territory.

"Mom! Add the scented beads to the bath while the water is running, not after the tub is full! Start over or I won't have the right bubbles!

"Mom! Where did you go? Come talk to me while I'm bathing! And bring my relaxation CD. Not that one! The blue one! Blue! Now turn it up. Not that loud!

"Mom! Rub in my sparkle lotion so it's even. Not up and down! Rub in the direction of natural hair growth!

"Mom! Put my pantyhose on me, because my fingernails are still wet. And don't smudge my sparkle lotion!

"Mom! My new shoes are slick on the bottom! Take them outside and rough them up on the driveway!

"Mom . . ."

When Allison and her date finally walked out the door, the house settled into an uneasy silence. Sort of like the quiet following four hours of continuous buzz-saw noise.

Then clarity hit.

I ran to the driveway, calling to Allison, "Have a good time, sweetheart! And stay out *as long and as late as you want*!"

I was only thinking of her.

She Says . . .

Allison (daughter)

Whoever came up with "Don't sweat the small stuff" was never a girl getting ready for high school prom, or he'd know there's no such thing as "small stuff." Girls are so stressed out. Our periods go wacky and we get all bloaty and PMS-y and our faces break out, so we have to pay extra for rush shipping on a pore vacuum from an infomercial that we saw at 2:00 a.m. when we were trying to highlight our own hair to save money for our prom dress.

Sorry. Had to vent.

But every year, things go wrong that are impossible to plan for. Like the first time I got ready for prom and my regular hair stylist wasn't available, so a new one almost ruined my hair. I pretended to like it so she wouldn't feel bad, but when we got home I freaked out, so Mom redid it and then I felt better.

The next year I wanted to have nice fingernails, so on prom afternoon I bought a kit for a French-tip manicure. But the nails kept going crooked because the glue wouldn't dry, so Mom had to put my pantyhose on me. She never complained, but it was still just weird.

Guys have it easy because they just have to shave and show up. Although one year, after all the trouble I went through to look nice, my date arrived in a new shirt still crinkled from being folded in the package. He looked like a Dumpster diver, and it ticked me off. But Mom ironed his shirt, and then he looked really nice.

The pressure for a perfect prom was gi–normous, especially my senior year when I was nominated for queen. Everything went great until time to put my dress on. It was a tight, straight dress with spaghetti straps and no zipper, which made it almost impossible to get over my head without ruining my hair. But Mom somehow slipped it on, and I felt beautiful.

Prom is supposed to be glamorous and romantic, but all I remember is feeling overwhelmed, like everything was happening too fast while going wrong at the same time on what should be a Cinderella-at-the-ball night. My mom was always right there to help me, and if we were together right this minute, I'd have just one thing to ask her to do: "Hold me."

How Would You Deactivate the Daughter's Bossy Button?

a. Impose hefty fines on high schools that schedule prom anywhere near Allison's period (or Diana's if she's not shocked into early menopause).

b. Petition to replace formal proms with hayrides that include automatic suspension for any student violating the dress code of jeans and flannel shirts.

c. Avoid future school dances by pulling Allison out of high school to get her GED.

Debi Says . . .

Dear Diana,

Prom preparations can be stressful. But shopping for a dress, getting an updo, and being nominated for queen are nothing compared to being on the publicity committee, the decorating committee, *and* the cleanup committee because everyone else was too cool to show a little school spirit and the only guy who asked you to dance was the retiring history teacher with a bad hip. Not that it ever happened to me.

So let me commend you for being patient with Allison. She's an extremely likable and beautiful young woman who, under normal circumstances, is thoughtful and considerate. But prom is not a normal circumstance. I'm proud of you for not choosing one of the most pressurized nights of her life to give her an attitude lecture. That's gotta happen the month before. Repeatedly.

I'm certain you educated Allison about menstruation before her first period arrived. So describe what happens to women before a big event: panicky thoughts, sleep troubles, last-minute problems. A trial run of getting ready might also help calm Allison's nerves. Today it's prom, but tomorrow it could be a job interview, a college term paper, or a formal corporate dinner.

If she's lucky, like some outstandingly gifted people who succeeded in spite of bad prom memories, it could even be a book signing at Wal-Mart.

God Says . . .

"Forget about self-confidence; it's useless. Cultivate God-confidence" (1 Corinthians 10:12 MSG).

Help Me Say . . .

Dear Lord, you know a big event can test any woman's nerves—including mine. Remind me that bossiness often camouflages fear. Help me to teach my daughter that confidence doesn't come from how she looks but in whose she is: yours. Amen.

"She's So Dramatic!"

· *Chapter 14* ·

THE ELABORATOR

I got my hair highlighted, because I felt some strands were more important than others.

—Anonymous

She Says . . .

Debi (mother)

If Arnold Schwarzenegger is known as "The Terminator," then my daughter, Elizabeth, is "The Elaborator." Her penchant for complexity turns the simplest of tasks into expansive productions. Say I'm scrambling eggs for breakfast and ask her to serve some fruit. I'm thinking *bowl of apples.* But Elizabeth is thinking *apples, oranges, grapes, strawberries, cantaloupe, mangoes, bananas, and kiwi served in hand-sculpted watermelon.*

Elizabeth has always liked her life to be as colorful and chaotic as possible. Take a recent evening when she asked me to help dye her hair.

"Sure!" I said. We'll goop the color on her head, make girl talk while it sets, then rinse it out. Thirty minutes, tops. Definitely doable and possibly fun.

When I met her in the bathroom, she had a box of hair dye in each hand.

"Trying to decide which color to use?" I asked.

"No. One is for highlights."

"Really? Who's putting those in for you?"

"You are."

"Me? I don't know how to do highlights!"

"It's easy. My friends do theirs all the time."

"Then call one of them! I don't know how to do highlights!"

"They're busy. Besides, I need my hair done before Jennifer's party tomorrow."

Elizabeth showed great faith by asking me to do this. When she was little and depended on me to style her hair, she had limited options: one ponytail or two. Highlighting hair was so far out of my comfort zone, it would need a passport to visit me.

Yet for the sake of quality girl time and to keep my promise, I calmed myself. Then I saw the foil.

"Elizabeth, why is foil in the bathroom?"

"For wrapping my highlights."

"Like in the salon?"

"Mom, relax. You can do it."

"Do it? I thought I was *helping*—as in dabbing drips off your neck!"

"It's not that big of a deal, Mom."

"Excuse me! It's a huge deal that should've been started hours ago—*by a professional*! At this rate, we'll be up half the night!"

"No, we won't. We're going to dye and highlight at the same time."

"At the same time! Are you insane? I don't know how to do any of this!"

Three and a half hours later, we finished. The bathroom (and our clothes) would need industrial applications of bleach to get them clean again, but Elizabeth's hair looked fantastic. Then, at that late hour, my beautiful social butterfly wanted to keep the fun going with a detailed discussion on what kind of wedding she'll have someday.

"I want something simple, Mom, but definitely an ice sculpture. . . ."

Lord, have mercy.

She Says . . .

Elizabeth (daughter)

As different as my mother and I are, we are both high maintenance.

Emotionally, I need lots of hugs and love and attention and hugs and presents and love and hugs and jewelry and hugs and flowers and love and DVDs and hugs. My mom is like a goldfish. Just change the water and feed her a few pellets (a.k.a. hugs) now and again, and she is a happy little swimmer.

My mother's high-maintenance personality kicks in at restaurants. She can't order a simple meal and be done with it. She has special instructions for her drink, her salad, and her entrée. Her excuse for this dining drama? "I waited tables during my years as a student. It's the server's job to make me happy, not my job to make his life easy." But I'm totally low maintenance about what I wear in public. Give me a sassy T-shirt, comfy sleep pants, and flip-flops, and I'm dressed for the day.

Recently, I wanted to try a more polished look: blue, purple, and black dreadlocks. Since I was searching for a job, though, I decided to go with the tamer choice of black hair with burgundy streaks. I had been planning this for weeks, and the next day was a friend's party. So I asked my mom if she would mind helping me.

That was my first mistake. I should have made a

typed, step-by-step plan in triplicate with color-coded tabs in D-ring binders and submitted them to her two months in advance after bribing her with chocolate.

Mom agreed to help me but needed "just a minute" to check her e-mail first. An hour and a half later, she appeared in the bathroom doorway with a shriek.

"*What* is all *that*?"

Mom always complains that I don't plan ahead, but this time I had: old towels to protect our clothes, petroleum jelly to smooth around my hairline, and foil to wrap the burgundy streaks while black dye soaked the rest of my hair. Did she not see any of that?

"Elizabeth, I thought you only needed help!"

"Yeah, I do only need help. Help applying it. I'm not double-jointed."

Mom begrudgingly helped me. My hair turned out great and I got tons of compliments, but apparently all future episodes of spontaneity must be scheduled in advance.

How Would You Deactivate the Daughter's Dramatic Button?

a *Saturation therapy.* Immerse Elizabeth in overstimulation by making her ride an indoor roller coaster in a garish Vegas hotel lobby with flashing lights and noisy slot machines while holding a bundle of lit sparklers in each hand and talking on two cell phones. No, wait. She'd probably like that.

b *Reverse psychology.* Teach Elizabeth simplicity by making her live in a remote convent for one year. No, wait. Cruelty to nuns is illegal.

c *Free association.* Give Elizabeth away to any association willing to take her.

Debi Says . . .

Dear Reader,

I wish I knew your name. "Reader" seems so cold. Why don't each and every one of you write to me so I can insert your names? That will give this part of the story a more personal feel; plus, it will buy time before my friends point out my blind spots again:

- "The first mistake was being asked. The second, succumbing under pressure! Were you insane or was Elizabeth? I colored my daughter's hair once, and she has never forgiven me."
- "When a gal wants to dye her hair, be thankful. It means she can handle risk and live with unpredictable outcomes."
- "Props to Elizabeth for believing her mom could do this without a total hair disaster! There is obviously a great deal of trust and confidence in your mother-daughter relationship."
- "Don't freak out at Elizabeth's last-minute embellishments of life. She's not wrong; she's just different. Sure, she could tone down the drama and work on her planning skills, but you need to loosen up."

God Says . . .

"Don't pick on people, jump on their failures, criticize their faults—unless, of course, you want the same treatment. That critical spirit has a way of boomeranging" (Matthew 7:1–2 MSG).

Help Me Say . . .

Oh, Lord! I could get along with my daughter so much easier if she were more like *me*. Oops. You just pointed out that we could both get along better if we were each more like *you*. Good point, God. Please reprogram my responses to my daughter so that they are less critical and more encouraging. Amen.

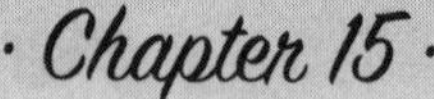

TIARAS FOR TWO

Kathleen: People do really stupid
things in foreign countries.
Frank: Absolutely. They buy leather jackets
for much more than they're worth.

—You've Got Mail, *by Nora Ephron*

She Says . . .

Carol (mother)

I was a starry-eyed newlywed on my first European tour. This trip held the promise of romance, beauty, romance, history, romance, art, and . . . teenagers.

After I married Darrall, a senior chief in the navy, he took my fifteen-year-old daughter, Christine, and me with him to his new station in Stuttgart, Germany. There he offered to treat us to a European tour by bus. To appease Christine and to give us some breathing room, we invited her friend Jenny along.

Imagine taking a moonlit gondola ride in Venice. Romantic, right? But Darrall and I were being followed by two teenage girls! Christine later made an embarrassing scene about the canals being unsanitary when all I wanted to do was bask in the afterglow of the gondola ride. I tuned her out completely when she started ranting about exposure to the bubonic plague.

In Florence, one of our tour's first stops was a quaint shopping district. The tour guide popped open his red umbrella (our beacon in case we got lost) and announced a special surprise: the famous leather shop he had been telling us about was just around the corner.

I'll never forget walking in that door and seeing wall-to-wall leather: vests, purses, belts, hats, jackets, briefcases, and boots. And the smell! So rich and sophisticated, so classy and alluring, so soft and—*gasp*! Then I saw it: the coat.

Beautifully crafted black leather, hip length, with detailed embossing on the sleeves, a silk paisley lining, and huge padded shoulders. (Hey, it was the '80s.) Darrall held my purse while I tried it on. When I brought that long, silver zipper up to my neck, I knew my destiny: to wear fine Italian leather for the rest of my life. Darrall insisted on buying it as an early anniversary present. Being a submissive wife, I didn't argue.

When Christine found out, she demanded a leather coat too. Darrall said the day's budget couldn't cover two coats but he'd buy her one later. Besides, we still needed money for lunch.

"But Mom's getting one now," she whined. "It's not fair!"

"Christine," I said, "this is my anniversary present. It's not your anniversary, so you're not getting a present."

"I don't want a present. I want a coat. A leather coat from Italy."

You'd think we were denying her oxygen, but we did not give in, not even when she pouted all through lunch at that little Italian café. What a prima donna!

She Says . . .

Christine (daughter)

I've heard my mom tell this story, but she doesn't do it right. It wasn't even her and Darrall's first anniversary but their second. Not that it makes any difference, because they were still acting like newlyweds.

Like in Venice when we took gondola rides. My friend Jenny and I followed Mom and Darrall. They were all cuddled up and kissing under the bridges and listening to the guy with the stick serenading them. How could they not smell the stench of the canals? They were nasty! Jenny and I saw garbage and dead rats floating next to us, but all Mom and Darrall could do was smile all lovey-dovey. Gag!

At least when we rode the tour bus we didn't have to watch them. Jenny and I scrunched down in our seats to talk, play cards, and listen to tapes of U2 and Oingo Boingo on our headsets. Sleeping on the bus made us feel all rumpled in the morning. So when we pulled into Florence, Jenny and I wanted to go to the hotel to shower and change clothes. But no, we had to stay with the group. I mean, this trip was so unfairly slanted toward the adults.

Jenny and I followed my mom into a leather shop. I'll never forget walking in and being choked by the over-powering smell of treated leather. It was awful! Besides that, the tiny shop, packed with tourists, was making me claustrophobic.

Mom started twirling around in this leather coat that was actually kind of nice, but I didn't think she'd get it; it was too expensive. But she was all goo-goo eyed, and when Darrall said he would buy it for her, she started squealing and hopping up and down. She gets so dramatic over shopping, it's embarrassing sometimes.

Honestly, I didn't care whether or not Darrall bought her a coat, but I put my foot down when he said it would take all of our money for the rest of the day. That was so unfair. Did my mother expect everyone to suffer and miss meals just so she could have her precious coat? Apparently. I felt really embarrassed that Jenny, who was our guest, had to sacrifice for my mom's coat.

Besides, I had always wanted to experience one of those little Italian cafés, and she had just killed my dream.

How Would You Deactivate the Mother's and Daughter's Dramatic Buttons?

a. Teach them to say, "C'est la vie" ("That's life," in Italian).

b. Physically separate Carol and Christine until their agents work out details for their dressing rooms and stunt doubles.

c. Offer free gelato for whoever mimics the European emergency siren better.

Debi Says . . .

Dear Carol,

It's a tie for "Best Actress in a Stressful Role."

As a newlywed mom with a personality opposite of her teenage daughter, you (and your daughter) were hormonal and off-kilter from traveling. Christine is a laid-back, logical thinker who notices all the details, while you're a happy gal who likes to have fun and follow shiny objects. C'mon, Carol. You'll dance for joy in public if you have a two-for-one chalupa coupon. No wonder you clashed!

Still, when you looked back on this international incident during our interview, you had some great insight for the next vacation for you and your daughter:

- Pray together each morning.
- Plan ahead how much to spend on meals, lodging, gifts, etc.
- Don't buy so impulsively that all the money is spent the first day.

Christine was only acting her age but could have benefited from a gentle rebuke: "Sweetheart, this is Darrall's gift to me. His gift to you is the pleasure of your friend's company for the entire trip. This argument is officially over, and we are now going to enjoy the rest of the day."

One more tip: report that tour guide to Interpol, because I think he was getting a kickback from the leather shop.

God Says . . .

"Each of you should look not only to your own interests, but also to the interests of others" (Philippians 2:4 NIV).

Help Me Say . . .

Dear God, forgive me for taking center stage. Sometimes I get so caught up in the fun of the moment that I overlook or minimize what my daughter is feeling. Please help me filter my emotions so I can respond to her with sensitivity, firmness, and grace. Amen.

· *Chapter 16* ·

CAUTION: HORMONES AHEAD!

Admitting you have a problem is the first step toward getting medicated for it.

—Jim Evarts

She Says . . .

Julie (mother)

It started the morning I took Melanie, who's fourteen, to the doctor. I have to amuse myself in waiting rooms, particularly now that I'm an easily irritated, premenopausal woman. The pediatrician's office is the only place with *Highlights for Children* magazine, and circling the hidden objects in the big picture always calms me down. But all the hidden objects in the picture were already circled. How rude! Now I had nothing to do. And the waiting room was way too hot. Did I mention that I'm premenopausal?

Melanie showed no sympathy. I was bored, ignored, miffed, overheated, and something else, but I don't remember what it was.

After the appointment, we left to do errands and have lunch. Melanie didn't help my mood by playing her CD in the car at a window-rattling level. When the CD started skipping, her solution was to whack the CD player. *Whack it!* Where she could've learned such impulsive, hormonally imbalanced behavior is beyond me. When her whacking activated blinking lights on the car, I reached my limit.

"What are those lights, Melanie? Turn them off!"

"I didn't turn 'em on! You did!"

"I did not! You did it by whacking the CD player!"

"I did not! You did it by whacking the steering wheel!"

Because I am premenopausal, I pulled into a parking lot with a screech. The tires also made a noise.

Melanie leaned to her left and fidgeted around the steering wheel to find whatever button she thought *I* had pushed. I leaned to the right and felt all around the CD player to see how *she* had triggered the lights. Meanwhile, we yelled, the music blared, and those stupid lights blinked like strobes in a disco.

Mike, my husband, teases Melanie and me about being goofballs and getting in a jam every time we go out. We tried to avoid calling him for help again but finally gave in. Turns out the hazard lights can be deactivated by pushing a little triangular button—and yes, it's by the steering wheel, but I am premenopausal and may need bifocals, so what of it?

The day was ruined. Ruined beyond all repair. What's the point in doing errands and having lunch on a totally ruined day? My only recourse: head home like a crazed NASCAR driver, slam a few doors, and pout in solitude.

With chocolate.

She Says . . .

Melanie (daughter)

When Mom is in my doctor's waiting room, she wants one thing: *Highlights for Children* magazine. Not to read to me, though. I'm too old for it. But apparently she, at age forty-two, is not. She likes to circle the hidden objects in the big picture. It's really embarrassing.

So I sat in a corner, listening to loud music on my headphones. Then Mom jumped into view and started hopping and pointing. Her face was red and her mouth moved a lot, but I couldn't understand her. It was kind of funny until she lunged for my headphones. Then I knew she meant business.

"Mo-om! I'm trying to listen to my music."

"Melanie! Didn't you hear me? There's only one *Highlights* magazine, and some kid already circled the hidden objects!"

"So?"

"So? *So?* That's all you can say? Don't you care? Circling the hidden objects is my special treat when I come here, and some kid ruined it!"

"So?"

"Quit saying 'So'! Now what am I supposed to do?"

"Calm down, Mom. You're embarrassing me." I pointed

to a table covered in magazines for grown-ups. "Why don't you go over there and get something else to read?"

"I don't want those. I want *Highlights*."

Mom pouted, refusing to read anything. Yeah, right. Like *that* will teach everyone not to mess with her *Highlights* magazine.

Afterward, in the car, my CD started skipping, so I whacked the stereo. Sometimes that fixes it. But then Mom starting screaming about lights flashing. I thought maybe a cop was pulling her over or she was hallucinating about UFOs.

"Turn off the lights! Turn off the lights!"

"Mom," I said, "there aren't any lights. We're driving in the daytime."

"The lights are blinking! The lights are blinking!"

It's like she was Paul Revere or something, saying everything twice.

From a parking lot, we called my dad, and he helped us fix the problem, as usual. I thought we could finally shop and have a nice lunch out, but no. Mom was so worked up and mad at me, she drove straight home without talking. I know speeding is illegal, and I'm pretty sure driving around corners on two wheels is too.

What should *really* be illegal is for mothers to be dramatic in public. It is so embarrassing.

How Would You Deactivate the Mother's Dramatic Button?

a Buy Julie a subscription to *Highlights for Children* and hide the issues until time for the next doctor's appointment.

b Applaud Julie's performance and then announce in a loud voice, "Folks, that's why she's been nominated for Most Embarrassing Mother in a Public Place."

c Whip out a video camera so you can play back Julie's diva scene to her later (but wear your running shoes while you're filming).

Debi Says . . .

Julie, Julie, Julie,

Where's a tranquilizer gun when you need it?

Hormonal days aren't a picnic for anyone, whether they're prepubescent panic attacks or premenopausal meltdowns. When we chatted (during which your normal, sweet self presided), you said, "I was too quick to speak and too quick to blame. I was not in a good frame of mind and didn't handle the situation well."

Yay! I applaud any mom who can admit her mistakes, especially in front of her daughter, as you did. That puts you well on the road to avoiding another drama-rama.

Now that you realize venting at everyone (and possibly stripping the transmission in your car) is not good, have you considered seeing your doctor? Investigating natural supplements to help with mood swings, hot flashes, and memory lapses? Getting more sleep? Meditating on soul-soothing Scriptures?

When I say these things can help your moods before they spiral out of control, I'm speaking from experience. They make interacting with people easier, especially my family. I love them all so much (sniff). Elizabeth was the most adorable baby (sniff, sniff). Excuse me (sniff). I need to get a tissue.

God Says . . .

"But when the Holy Spirit controls our lives, he will produce this kind of fruit in us: love, joy, peace, patience, kindness, goodness, faithfulness, gentleness, and self-control. Here there is no conflict with the law" (Galatians 5:22–23 NLT).

Help Me Say . . .

Lord, help! My attempts at self-control are not working. I need *your* patience, *your* kindness, *your* gentleness. Otherwise I end up hurting the people I love the most. Please nudge me, knock on the door of my heart, and remind me that calmness—not drama—comes from letting you take charge. Amen.

Conclusion

Last to Leave the Party

> Life may not be the party we hoped for, but while we're here we should dance.
>
> —*Anonymous*

OK, girlfriend. Everyone else has left the party, so it's just you and me. Let's kick off our shoes, compare toe rings, and talk more freely.

Like most women, you and I probably don't have dramatically abusive histories with our mothers and daughters. What we *do* have are recurring conflicts that are irritating or puzzling rather than explosive or painful. So when these conflicts erupt, what's the first thing we do (after putting all sharp objects out of reach)?

Natural reactions—those that come without forethought or choice—aren't always helpful. Pouting. Screaming. Nagging. Stuffing. Calling friends for sympathy. Following talk-show advice. Slinging Bible verses. Bringing up past offenses. Giving the silent treatment. Binging on ice cream. Indeed, these are not pretty. They're even less effective at moving us toward our goal of healthy relationships.

What we need, then, is not a natural reaction but a supernatural one—a reaction that is not human but holy.

Personally, I only have so much patience. It fluctuates based on how much sleep I had, the traffic I faced, and the stress I battled. So when my patience is gone, it's gone. Same for my wisdom, my kindness, my love, and so on. That's why I am desperate for God in my life. When I opened the door of my heart to Jesus Christ and said, "It's a mess, but come on in," everything changed.

Now when my personal resources are insufficient (which is pretty much 24-7), I can plug into God's resources. He has patience to spare and delights in sharing it with us (Romans 15:5). Ditto with wisdom (James 1:5), kindness (Psalm 86:15), and love (1 John 4:7). These qualities and more are crucial to resolving conflicts of all shapes and sizes. That's why seeking his help is always the first step. Always.

What else do I recommend? Something taught to me by another wise person: look beyond the details and make peace with the big picture. This means that even if she (the mother or daughter in our life who's pushing our buttons) refuses to budge, we *choose* to focus not on that pesky pixel of a problem but on the panorama of our lifelong relationship.

Like the time Elizabeth and I brainstormed this book in my home office. I stood and taped sheets of paper to the wall with color-coded sticky notes to create a detailed overview of the book's organization. Elizabeth sat on the floor and used strips of tape to clean the pores on her nose. But months later, when we critiqued each other's writing, we were totally in sync. I told her, "Make me sound bossier." She told me, "Add more dialogue." We were *both* right.

Elizabeth and I will always love each other, and we will always be different. And as much as we enjoy each other's company, we can't avoid the occasional *argh!* moments of smotherly love. We may vent. We may complain. We may enter meltdown. But we don't stay angry. We don't feed our hurts. And we never withhold forgiveness.

Can you say the same?

If you can't, choose your favorite story in this book. Then call your mother or daughter and say, "Let me read this to you, and then tell me what you think." It's a great first step to a mother-daughter party of your own.